Original title:
A Journey to the Ocean's Depths

Copyright © 2025 Creative Arts Management OÜ
All rights reserved.

Author: Dorian Ashford
ISBN HARDBACK: 978-1-80587-353-2
ISBN PAPERBACK: 978-1-80587-823-0

A Dance with the Deep

The fish all wear their finest suits,
In underwater fancy boots.
They twirl and spin, so full of cheer,
While singing songs for all to hear.

A crab played drums upon a shell,
A mermaid danced, oh what the swell!
The seaweed swayed, it joined the fun,
As jellyfish glowed like setting sun.

They laughed at whales with silly hats,
While dolphins pranced like acrobats.
A starfish tried to join the beat,
But ended up just stuck in seat.

With bubbles popping, cheers were loud,
The ocean floor became a crowd.
They all agreed, with glee and gaff,
That dancing deep is quite a laugh!

Beneath Waves of Time

A turtle told a tall tale beast,
Of laughing squids, and clam-filled feasts.
With tales of treasure lost and found,
He winked and spun, then tumbled round.

An octopus with juggling skills,
Balanced shells with swirls and frills.
As fish swam by, they giggled loud,
For sea life art was quite a crowd.

A dolphin hiccuped, shot some foam,
While sea cucumbers called it home.
They planned a show for all to see,
With fishy magic called "Oh Me!"

The audience roared with water's glee,
As bubbles popped in jubilee.
In ocean's halls where laughter stays,
They danced and played for endless days.

Temptation of the Trench

The fish are getting fancy, wearing pearls,
Dancing like they know the latest swirls.
I reached for one, and then I fell,
Right into a seaweed-covered shell.

The crabs all laughed, "What a sight!"
With a pinch and a crack, I took flight.
I swear those clams just winked at me,
But I was too busy, stuck in a spree.

Underwater Labyrinths

In a maze of kelp, I lost my way,
Dolphins giggled, wanted to play.
I turned left, then right, what a goofy move,
Only to find a snail in the groove.

The sea cucumbers were quite the sight,
Waving their arms, oh what a delight!
They whispered secrets of the deep,
But all I got was a fishy peep.

The Coral Kingdoms' Secret

In coral castles, mermaids sip tea,
They laughed at my fins, said, "Look at he!"
With crowns of shells, they danced around,
While I tripped on sand, belly to ground.

"Join our court!" they cheerfully sang,
But I sneezed so loud, they just banged.
A crab in a tuxedo took a bow,
I didn't quite fit in, oh dear, oh wow!

In Search of Neptune's Treasures

I followed a map marked with fishy cues,
Found a treasure chest with nothing but blues.
I scratched my head, thought I might cry,
When I opened it up and got a fish pie.

Neptune chuckled from his oceanic chair,
"Try my trident, if you dare!"
But it poked my fin, oh what a laugh,
I splashed around, had the best gaff!

Stranded in Celestial Waters

Floating high on fluffy waves,
I waved to dolphins in their caves.
They laughed at me, a silly sight,
With sunscreen slathered, oh so bright.

A crab approached, took my flip-flop,
He scuttled off, I thought to stop.
But chasing crabs is quite a blunder,
I tripped on seaweed, what a thunder!

The fish all giggle as I flail,
I yell, "A little help! I'm off the scale!"
They offered spices, made me stew,
But I can't cook! Oh, what to do?

In this sea of pranksters, I reside,
With jellyfish my silly guide.
We toast with shells as stars align,
In celestial waters, life's divine!

Secrets of the Forgotten Depths

Bubbles rise from ancient tales,
Of sunken ships and ghostly whales.
I met a clam, he told me jokes,
About the sailors and their hoax!

There's treasure here, in frilly shells,
But watch out for those sneaky swells.
An octopus, quite wise and sly,
Offered me pearls, but oh my, why?

I tried to barter with my hat,
He said, "For that? I'll give you a pat!"
So here I swim in laughter's grip,
While mermaids giggle, I do a flip.

With every wave, a giggle's churned,
In the depths where laughter's learned.
Secrets swirl in salty glee,
This underwater jesting spree!

Farewell to the Surface

I waved goodnight to the land so bright,
As fish threw me a goofy light.
They spun and twirled in playful cheer,
While I just bobbed like a floating beer!

A seagull cawed, "You won't be back!"
I winked at him, "I'll ride this track!"
Each wave a tumble, a splashy dance,
As I embraced my ocean chance.

Whales joined in with a singing fleet,
Harmonizing, making my heart beat.
We danced beneath the swirling moon,
In the salty depths, I found my tune.

So farewell, surface, I'm lost in glee,
With creatures swirling around me.
In a sea of whimsy, I reside,
With waves of laughter as my guide!

Descend into Wonder

Down I go, with a splashy cheer,
As fish in tuxedos twirl near.
They pulled me in for a dance-off show,
With a crab DJ spinning below!

I tripped on seaweed, fell on my face,
But laughter echoed in the place.
Sea turtles joined with a funky swish,
Making waves of frothy bliss.

The jellyfish glowed in neon hues,
Playing games in their shiny shoes.
I tried to join, but stumbled a lot,
While laughing fish thought I was hot!

In this wonder, the ocean's embrace,
Fun and folly, a joyous race.
With every gurgle, every cheer,
I dwell in laughter, year after year!

Celestial Currents and Coral Canvases

The fish wear ties with style so slick,
A turtle's dancing, it's quite a trick.
Without a map, we roam and swim,
Chasing a seahorse named Jim.

Jellyfish waltz, they glow and drift,
While crabs play cards, oh what a gift!
The octopus juggles shells like a pro,
Making us laugh with his silly show.

In the depths where the sun's shy to peek,
Mermaids giggle, their laughter unique.
They trade seaweed for tales of woe,
In this underwater circus, we go with the flow.

So let's dive deep and paint the night,
With coral brushes, colors so bright.
In the kingdom where bubbles form,
There's no dull moment, only fun is the norm.

Willows of the Sea

In water like silk, the willows sway,
Fish complain, it's another long day.
A crab's on the mic telling the news,
While eels make jokes that always amuse.

Anemones dance with their wiggle and spin,
Telling the shrimp, "Hey, come join in!"
Starfish audition for a Broadway play,
But they just sit there, being quite gray.

The seaweed winks, a gossiping sage,
Whale songs echo like a comedy stage.
Fins slap together, like applause in tune,
Under the laughter of a glowing moon.

So let's prance with the dolphins, so cheery and spry,
With bubbles and giggles, we'll reach for the sky.
The ocean's a place for quirky delight,
Where every adventure sparks laughter at night.

Harmonies of the Deep

Bubble blowing contests, who can rip?
A fish with a hat just took a dip.
Sardines in a band play tunes so sweet,
While sea cucumbers tap their feet.

The angler fish shines with a light so bright,
Texting his friends, "Let's meet tonight!"
Echoing laughter from the depths below,
Makes sea stars giggle, 'Oh, don't be so slow!'

Tangled in sea grass, a crab's stuck real tight,
Trying to dance, what a comical sight!
Grouper make jokes about weather and waves,
While dolphins swim by, bringing fresh raves.

In underwater festivals, we cheer and shout,
With bubbles and laughs, there's never a doubt.
For the ocean's a stage, where silliness flows,
In the depths of the sea, pure joy overflows.

The Unseen Voyage

Behind the reef, what's lurking there?
A narwhal's brushing, no need for a care.
He's creating art with a splash and a twirl,
While sea lions cheer, giving a whirl.

The sand tells tales of a lost shoe,
What is life like without a view?
Shrimp in tuxedos parade up and down,
Making the fish laugh, "Oh, what a clown!"

An octopus spins like a top, oh what speed,
"Catch me if you can!" is his daring creed.
But tangled in kelp, he gets quite hot,
Yelling, "Next time, I'll just stay in my spot!"

So under the waves, we frolic and play,
Where laughter bubbles in a silly display.
In the unseen parts, where the treasures hold,
Every fish tale is a joy to be told.

The Enigmas of Trench Waters

In the dark where fish wear hats,
And octopuses dance with bats.
Mermaids giggle, not a care,
While clams take selfies, unaware.

The sharks all joke; they've got their bite,
But here in the deep, it's purely light.
With bubbles floating all around,
They tease the divers making sounds.

Surprises lurk in every shell,
Like pirate jokes we all know well.
The seaweed sways, a joyful friend,
As jellyfish play tag, no end.

So dive on down, don't be too shy,
Join the fun, wave your worries bye!
In these trenches, laughter flows,
Among the gags that water knows.

Echoes and Currents

With gurgling laughs and splashes loud,
The fish parade, they're quite the crowd.
A whale drops puns, his voice a boom,
While starfish toss confetti in the gloom.

The currents swirl, they tickle toes,
As silly creatures strike a pose.
A dolphin winks; he's quite the tease,
Tickling sea cucumbers with ease.

Bubbles form, like laughter bright,
Blowing through the ocean's night.
Seahorses trot with tiny grins,
In this wet world, everyone wins.

So heed the echoes—join the cheer,
For down below, fun's always near!
Let the waves giggle, let them hum,
In the underwater, we're all just fun!

Dreaming in Shades of Blue

In shades of azure, fish do dream,
With coral crowns, they reign supreme.
A playful laugh from down below,
Where bubbles pop and sea fans blow.

A clownfish jokes, he paints the scene,
While turtles dance—their moves are keen.
Every wave holds a secret or two,
Of jokes shared 'neath the ocean's blue.

So let's don our fins, dive and glide,
Chasing giggles on the tide.
In every crevice, a chuckle is found,
Across the deep, let laughter abound!

From sandy shores to darkest depths,
We find the humor, ocean's steps.
Embrace the waves, join in the spree,
For who knew the sea could be so funny?

Ocean's Heartbeat

The ocean sings, a funny tune,
With crabs doing the cha-cha in the moon.
Clams all giggle, they just can't stop,
While fish throw parties at the coral shop.

The tides are in a jolly mood,
As seagulls join in, feasting on food.
The waves, they laugh—what a delight!
As dolphins play tag through the night.

In the deep, where shadows tease,
Eels spin around with utmost ease.
The seaweed jokes, it sways with flair,
As shrimp tell tales of their wild affair.

So listen close, can you hear it beat?
The ocean's heart—both lively and sweet!
Where silliness blooms beneath the foam,
And all water creatures feel right at home.

Sunken Pathways of Time

Down where the fish wear top hats,
And jellyfish dance with glee,
A clam named Larry sings show tunes,
While the sea cucumber drinks sweet tea.

The sea snails race on their shells,
With sparkles of bubbles in the air,
They chat about the latest tides,
And the best place to find a pear.

Turtles tell tales of lost socks,
Sponges write love letters to stars,
The octopus juggles seaweed,
As kids try to catch passing cars.

Dolphins dive in sequined suits,
Belting out pop songs all night,
While crabs criticize their moves,
Claiming only they get it right.

Tales from the Forgotten Ship

On a ship called S.S. Sillyhead,
Lived a captain with a pet shrew,
They'd dance on the deck every hour,
To the rhythm of a pirate crew.

Fish would provide snarky comments,
As seagulls squashed their grape juice,
The ship turned into a party,
With laughter, mayhem, and some moose.

Mermaids would sneak in to listen,
With shells that glimmer like ice,
They'd throw a surprise lobster roast,
Complete with jokes and some rice.

But the ship had a terrible problem,
It leaked milk instead of the brine,
They drank it with cookies for dinner,
Calling it a maritime dine!

The Sea's Hidden Diaries

In the depth of coral caverns,
Fish keep secrets galore,
They jot down notes on seaweed,
About the things they adore.

A grouper writes about his crush,
On a parrotfish named Sue,
While a crab sketches a menu,
For when her friends come to chew.

The octopus holds a lecture,
On the art of fine ocean cuisine,
With recipes for sea urchin pie,
Plates made of kelp so keen.

But the diary of the dolphin,
Is all about their swim team,
With notes on who splashed the most,
In waves that gleam and beam.

Color of the Current

Oh, the hues below the waves,
A splash of purple, green, and blue,
The fish wear coats of every shade,
And glitter like they just flew through.

One fish claimed to be a rainbow,
While others laughed with glee,
They said, "You're just a goldfish,
With a very wild spree!"

A starfish painted polka dots,
Claiming it was all the rage,
While sea cucumbers debated,
If they could join the stage.

In a swirl of playful colors,
The currents danced and played,
A caper of the ocean's palette,
In the lagoon where joy was made.

Beneath the Surface

I left my towel on the shore,
Diving down for a little more.
A fish with glasses waved hello,
"Do you have snacks?" I said, "Just dough!"

My flip-flop floated right on by,
Fish laughed as I started to cry.
They danced around my missing shoe,
While singing tunes, my face turned blue.

A crab approached with dancing flair,
And offered me his wooden chair.
I took a seat, but what a sight!
His buddies thought it was a fright!

So down I went, in a bubbly mess,
The ocean floor, I must confess,
Is full of jokes and fishy glee,
No Wi-Fi here, just laughs for me.

Submarine Reveries

In a sub that looked like a big tin can,
I found a fish with a top hat and a fan.
"What brings you here?" he asked with glee,
"Just trying to catch a wave of mystery!"

With a swish and a swirl, we went for a spin,
I grabbed a snack, and I tried to grin.
The bubble machine made it hard to breathe,
But giggles erupted, oh would they believe!

I told a joke; he didn't get the punch,
Instead, he offered me a seaweed lunch.
"It's quite gourmet, a little chewy,"
I said, "No thanks, I prefer my sushi!"

But laughter echoed through the steel walls,
As we made friends with octopuses in stalls.
Life beneath waves, a riotous thing,
With saltwater humor, and zingy bling.

Where Currents Converge

I sailed where the fish wear funny hats,
Met a dolphin who fancied spats.
"Come join my dance!" he smiled so wide,
"Just watch your step, it's a slippery ride!"

A starfish sat on a coral throne,
Asking me to lend him my phone.
"I need to call my crustacean friend,
To see if this party will ever end!"

The jellyfish floated by like a star,
Chasing bubbles that drifted afar.
"Let's have a race!" one flashed with cheer,
But I came last, thanks to my beer!

The sea's got jokes, and salty fun,
With currents that twist, and tides that run.
I waved goodbye to the waves of glee,
And swam back with a smile, not looking back at me.

Voyage to the Depths

With fins like flippers, oh what delight,
I swam with pirates who danced all night.
They taught me to jig on the ocean's floor,
Until I slipped and went out the door!

The squids wore shades, oh what a sight,
They told me, "Join, it's a slippery night!"
But as I flailed and bobbed about,
They laughed, "That's just how we swim about!"

"Grab the treasure, it's made of cheese,"
They yelled as I dodged the cloned sea peas.
I reached for gold but found a boot,
"Looks like you've unearthed a fashion dispute!"

With fishy puns echoing through the blue,
I learned that laughter's the best thing to do.
So off I swam, back to the shore,
With tales of whimsy, who could ask for more?

Vow of the Deep Sea

Sandy crabs dance in a line,
While fish argue over the best brine.
A turtle in specs, quite a sight,
Claims he's the captain; oh, what a fright!

Starfish debating who shines the most,
Squid in a suit, playing the host.
With laughter bubbles rising so high,
An octopus giggles, 'I can fly!'

Jellyfish jiggle, oh what a show,
Swaying and swaying, to and fro.
They'd throw a party, but who's got the cake?
Mollusks just munch, for goodness' sake!

In depths unknown, joy reigns supreme,
All sea creatures chase the same dream.
With a wink and a wave, they roam free,
Who knew the ocean could be so goofy?

Glimmers of the Abyss

In the dark, where the sun won't simmer,
Glowworms twinkle like stars' glimmer.
A fish with a flashlight, doing a tour,
'Everywhere I go, it's just more and more!'

Eels make up rhymes, strike silly poses,
While clams crack jokes, as laughter dozes.
'Why did the crab always cross the sea?'
He wanted to get to the other tea!

Drifting with bubbles, the laughs never end,
A pirate shark, his treasure to spend.
He found a lost sock, now quite the claim,
'I'll wear it with pride, I'll bring you fame!'

Mermaids gossip, over shells they chat,
'Did you hear about the chatty old cat?'
Tales of the oddities down below,
Where even the seaweed sways to and fro!

The Great Blue Expanse

Splendidly floating on waves of delight,
Fish pull pranks; oh, what a sight!
A whale on a skateboard, rolling by fast,
'Look at me now, I'm in the cast!'

Corals in colors, so bright and bold,
Create a canvas with stories untold.
Seahorses giggle, in pairs they dance,
'This ocean life is such a romance!'

A crab's birthday bash, with friends all around,
Octopuses juggling, displaying their talent.
They sing till the dawn, a wild serenade,
With clam cakes and mussels, all nicely laid.

As the sun sinks low, the laughter won't cease,
Even the waves breathe a sigh of peace.
When diving in dreams, how funny it seems,
Life underwater is all about schemes!

Rift Between Light and Dark

At the edge of light, where the shadows play,
A dolphin spins tales of the bright next bay.
Algae tickle and tease in styling their hair,
While sea turtles giggle without a care.

Shimmering critters in confusing ballet,
Flipping and flopping, as they make their way.
A crab yells, 'Hey, watch where you swim!'
Then trips on a seaweed, oh, isn't that grim?

Clownfish popping in and out of their home,
Making a mockery of their own foam.
'Why so serious?' asks a fish with a wink,
'Life's best fun is at the brink!'

So here in the deep, where the quirkiness roams,
Laughter abounds in the oceanic domes.
Though darkness may beckon and shadows may cast,
It's hilarious here, cheerfully vast!

Depths of the Deep Blue

With flippers on and goggles tight,
I dove right in, what a silly sight!
A fish with glasses swam by with glee,
"Hey there, buddy, you look like me!"

Bubbles floated up, making me giggle,
A dolphin danced, did a quirky wiggle.
"Dance with me!" he shouted with flair,
I twisted and twirled, without a care!

Then came a crab with a funky hat,
He pinched my shorts while I laughed at that.
"Hey, you! Don't take my stylish wear!"
He clapped his claws, with a mischievous stare.

At last, I found treasure, oh what a score!
Just candy wrappers... really, nothing more!
But the laughs we had, in watery delight,
Made the dive truly a comical sight!

Secrets of the Sunken Realm

Beneath the waves where laughter rings,
A mermaid giggles, shows off her blings.
"Look at my shells, they're quite the find!"
I couldn't help, I laughed and declined!

The octopus offered me a quick dance,
With eight wiggly limbs, oh what a chance!
He tripped on a rock, with a splash and a boom,
Sending fish flying, oh, how they zoom!

A clam in a corner was playing the lute,
But his music was really quite far from astute.
"Is that a tune or just a big flop?"
I couldn't stop chuckling — I had to stop!

When I asked a starfish if he could cheer,
He just lay still, said, "What's more sincere?"
Laughing with fish in this underwater show,
These secrets of laughter just stole the show!

Nautical Dreams

In nautical dreams, I took to the waves,
With a rubber duck, my fashion saves.
Mermaids were laughing, said I look fine,
"Just be yourself, there's no fashion line!"

A seagull swooped down, took my hat away,
"Come back, you thief!" I shouted in play.
He circled above, honking with pride,
As I splashed about, totally bonafide!

A fish with a top hat gave me a wink,
"You'll never guess what I like to drink!"
"Is it seaweed tea or kelp-flavored fizz?"
We giggled together, oh, what a whiz!

Then turtles arrived on an oversized boat,
"It's a slow ride, but we do it afloat!"
With goofy grins as we paddled so free,
These dreams of the sea felt silly to me!

Coral Kingdoms Unveiled

In coral kingdoms, bold and bright,
I found a crab who danced with delight.
"Come join my conga!" he shouted with glee,
But his two left feet made him trip — oh me!

Anemones waved like fans at a show,
"Take a bow, my friends, let's put on a glow!"
With fish in tuxedos and clownish charades,
We laughed till we cried at our silly cascades!

A lionfish strutted, full of pride,
"Check out my spikes, I'm quite the guide!"
But slipped on some sand, went tumbling down,
He mumbled and smiled, then chuckled around!

When I left the depths, with a grin ear to ear,
The coral planets clasped me with cheer.
In awkward ballet, and laughter galore,
This underwater party was hard to ignore!

Oceanic Labyrinths

In the deep, I took a dive,
Where fish wear shoes and crabs high-five.
I lost my map, oh what a sight,
Following a seahorse in the moonlight.

With jellyfish dancing like they're in a show,
I tried to tango, but stepped on a toe!
The starfish laughed, clapping their hands,
While I twirled in circles, lost in their bands.

An octopus winked with eight playful eyes,
I asked for directions; he just said 'surprise!'
So I rode on a turtle, all slow and steady,
As dolphins surfed, oh, they were so ready!

At last, I found treasures, all shiny and bright,
Turns out they were just gumdrops in the night.
I laughed with the sea, a fine happy chap,
In this ocean maze, I just needed a nap!

In the Arms of the Tides

The waves tickle toes like playful little critters,
While seahorses sing, oh how their voice jitters.
I tried to catch one, but it slipped right away,
Leaving me giggling, 'What a funny ballet!'

The sand crabs scuttled, making their burrows,
As I attempted a dance, but fell on my furrows.
'Who put this sand here?' I laughed through my coughs,
While the gulls overhead just pointed and scoffed.

In the arms of the tides, with seaweed as hair,
I made a new crown; I felt quite debonair!
A clam asked for fashion tips over some tea,
We chuckled at barnacles, oh, how they agree!

I floated away on a mattress of kelp,
My oceanic palace, I couldn't help yelp.
Mixing matches with fish in a bubble balloon,
Who knew the ocean could spark such a boon!

Murmurs from the Midnight Zone

In the midnight zone, where shadows creep,
I found some fish that just wouldn't sleep.
They told me jokes that made me roll,
With laughter resounding, oh what a toll!

A squid tried to paint, but oh, what a mess,
With colors of ink, he considered success!
But all he created was a big splat,
Leaving us chuckling, 'Well, imagine that!'

The anglerfish glowed, but was quite the tease,
He flicked his light, making everyone freeze.
With a wink and a grin, he made shadows dance,
And we all joined in for a goofy romance!

Down here in the deep, we cut loose and jest,
No proper etiquette, just laughter, no rest!
Sharing our stories, the deep sea's delight,
With murmurs and giggles, we owned the night!

Reflections in Saltwater

Gazing in saltwater, my face did appear,
With fish and a mermaid, giggling so clear.
'Is that really me?' I pondered aloud,
While she twirled around, so graceful and proud.

Bubble-blowing contests were all the rage,
The sea turtles joined in, a delightful stage.
I blew a big one; it popped with a splash,
The laughter erupted, oh what a crash!

With sea cucumbers wiggling about,
They shared their wise tales, without any doubt.
A clam chimed in, 'Now that's quite the catch!'
We joked 'bout the pearls, held tight in their hatch!

As the sun kissed the sea, I waved goodbye,
To fish in top hats, who bid me dry.
In reflections of salt, shared laughter does cling,
I swam back to shore, with joy on a swing!

Origins of Ocean Whispers

Bubbles rise, fish take flight,
A crab does a dance, what a sight!
Octopus juggles with a grin,
Underwater parties, let's begin!

Seashells gossip, whisper and sway,
Mermaids rolling in the spray,
A dolphin's laugh, a seahorse race,
Coral reefs hosting a silly space!

Starfish play hide and seek all day,
With sea cucumbers in a silly way,
Jellyfish glow, like disco lights,
But watch your step, avoid those bites!

Anemones tickle, squid throw a fit,
Lobsters wear suits, they're quite a hit!
The ocean's laughter, a bubbly cheer,
Come join the fun, there's nothing to fear!

Beneath the Undulating Surface

Waves tumble in with a splash and a squawk,
Clownfish giggle and play with a rock,
An eel wearing glasses, quite the sight,
Sardines in formation, they dance left and right!

A turtle slips by, a slow-motion glide,
While sea turtles chuckle, they cannot hide,
Penguins slipping on ice, oh what a show,
Each plunge into water is splendidly slow!

With crabs on the march, they strut with flair,
Pufferfish puffed up, unaware of the scare,
Dancing with kelp, tangled but sweet,
In this watery world, life's a treat!

The lobster sings songs, a jazzy affair,
Seahorses line dance, they've got real flair,
Fishy friends and giggles, what a delight,
Under the surface, it's party night!

Sand and Shadows of Time

The beach is calling with grains of gold,
Sandcastles rise, each story told,
A seagull courts a donut, quite a sight,
While crabs in tuxedos get ready to bite!

Footprints vanish with each gentle wave,
As seashells plot how to be brave,
Tides come and go, like a playful tease,
Starfish chuckles on a lazy breeze!

A beach ball bounces, with laughter it flies,
While sunscreen fights off the nosy spies,
Dune grass dances under the sun,
Chasing the shadows, oh, so much fun!

The horizon winks, the sunset's a mess,
Flip-flops forgotten, it's all for the best,
In the sand and shadows, memories blend,
A cheerful retreat, where worries suspend!

The Abyssal Whisperer

In the deep, where the lights grow dim,
A fishy bard sings a giddy hymn,
Whales play tag in a twisty embrace,
As shadows flit by, life's a wild race!

Ghostly shapes glide and put on a show,
An anglerfish grinning, ready to glow,
The abyss is alive with ridiculous flair,
A batfish struttin' with no need to care!

With a wink and a smile, the squid writes a tale,
Shapes in the darkness, a whimsy prevail,
Creatures unite in a raucous ballet,
In the depths of the ocean, let's dance today!

A crab shares secrets, the gossipy sort,
As jellyfish drift in a wobbly sport,
The abyssal whisperer keeps the fun deep,
Where laughter rises, and shadows leap!

The Submerged Odyssey

I strapped my fins, I'm feeling spry,
Just an average fish in a big old tie.
The octopus waved, with eight hands out,
"Come join the dance, without a doubt!"

I met a shark, who stole my snack,
He said, "Don't worry, I'll get you back!"
We swapped our woes, in bubbles we'd share,
Until a whale sneezed, and blew us in air!

Drowning in Celestial Waters

Stars above, a jellyfish moon,
I rode a seahorse, humming a tune.
Crabs played poker on the sandy floor,
While mermaids argued 'bout who buys more.

A dolphin laughed, with a splash so bright,
"Don't eat that kelp, it's quite the fright!"
I tried the sushi, it wiggled and glared,
Turns out seaweed should be well-prepared!

Visions of the Deep Sea

I dove too deep, lost my sense of fun,
Chasing bright fish, but oh, what a run!
A sea cucumber looked at me and sighed,
"Life's not a race, just take a glide!"

An anglerfish grinned, with a light on his head,
"You're in my territory, aren't you dead?"
We both just laughed 'til the bubbles ran wild,
Turns out deep sea life is often beguiled!

Reflections on the Ocean's Heart

I stumbled upon a treasure chest,
Filled with old socks, before I could rest.
A pirate declared, with a plank and a loot,
"These are my riches, so tie your own boot!"

We danced with the gulls, in a raucous ballet,
While crabs tap danced in an offbeat display.
The tide swept us up, on this salty parade,
Who knew the ocean would offer this grade?

Symphony of Submerged Stars

Underwater fish have quite the tune,
They dance and swish by the light of the moon.
Octopuses play instruments with flair,
While sea turtles groove without a care.

A clownfish cracks jokes in the coral reef,
With laughter echoing, you can't bequeath.
Starfish applaud with their five-pointed hands,
In this aquatic band, everyone stands.

Seahorses twirl in a dazzling line,
Bubbles burst forth like a party divine.
As whales take the stage with a deep bass sound,
The ocean's comedy show knows no bound.

Eels pull their tricks, zipping to and fro,
While they wiggle and giggle, putting on a show.
With every splash, the deep gives a cheer,
In this watery concert, there's always good cheer.

Tempests and Tranquility

Waves crash like a toddler's tantrum,
Seagulls squawk tales of oceanic wisdom.
With every gust, a ridiculous pose,
Sand flies in faces amidst the wind's blows.

Through storms, I see dolphins wearing shades,
Surfing the swells in their stylish parades.
A crab in a bowtie, oh what a sight,
Prepared for a gala beneath the moonlight.

As raindrops fall, they create little pools,
Where fish play hopscotch, bending the rules.
In calms, they trade tales of wild wind and spree,
A comedy of nature, this I must see!

So raise your glass, toast to storms and calm,
In oceanic chaos, we find our balm.
For laughter rides the waves, a joyous refrain,
In the tempest and peace, there's much to gain!

The Infinite Blue

I dipped my toes in a giant blue cup,
A jellyfish came up, said, "Hey, you wanna sit up?"
With a splash and a giggle, we spun around,
While deep-sea creatures gathered, music profound.

Turtles with shades jet-ski past my toes,
Waving hello as the ocean wind blows.
A fish in a top hat offered me a snack,
I laughed so hard, I nearly fell back!

In depths so vast, I spotted a ray,
Throwing parties for crustaceans in the bay.
With clam-shell cocktails and jokes by the shore,
The infinite blue never offered a bore!

As I floated along with my quirky pals,
We made splashy art with our underwater wails.
In this whimsical world, oh what a view,
In the laughter of fish, I found something true.

Depths of Enchantment

In caves where shadows twist and twine,
An octopus spins tales over a glass of brine.
Mermaids sip tea, and giggle below,
Unsure if the fish are just putting on a show.

With every swirl, a sea urchin grins,
As crabs play poker, letting the fun begin.
The depths hold laughter as bubbles arise,
Jellyfish juggle with amusing surprise!

Eels wear top hats, strutting with pride,
While seahorses race, oh what a wild ride!
Anemones prance in a floral ballet,
Where every wave whispers, "Come join the play!"

With a chuckle and splash, I embrace the sight,
The depths of enchantment are pure delight.
In this seashell world, let your worries sink,
For laughter is gold when we swim and think!

The Last Sunset on the Horizon

The sun dips low with a silly grin,
Fish wear shades, they dive right in.
The crabs all dance, doing a jig,
While sharks play cards, feeling quite big.

Seagulls laugh as they swoop and dive,
Telling fish tales that come alive.
A big wave splashes, a prankster's mark,
Leaving wet socks, oh what a lark!

The lighthouse winks, it knows the trick,
With beams that flash, a light-hearted flick.
Mermaids giggle, lost in the splash,
As pirates trip from a slippery crash.

As daylight fades, the laughter grows,
In the ocean's playground, anything goes!
The horizon yawns, one last big cheer,
As the ocean whispers, "Come back next year!"

Emerald Waters

In waters green where seaweed sways,
Clams play hide and seek all day.
Octopus juggles with graceful ease,
While turtles gossip beneath the trees.

Crabs wear hats, they're fashion bold,
As starfish pose like they're made of gold.
A dolphin sings a silly tune,
While fishes dance beneath the moon.

Bright corals hide treasure maps, so grand,
But the real prize? A heart-shaped sand.
With laughter echoing through the tide,
Emerald wonders are hard to hide.

The tides retreat, but laughter stays,
In this underwater world of plays.
From silly waves to playful spray,
Emerald waters brighten the day!

Hidden Wonders

Beneath the waves, a world unfolds,
Where jellyfish wear hats made of gold.
Seahorses trot in an elegant line,
Making sure they look simply divine.

Clownfish joke, 'We're the stars of the show!'
As they boast about how fast they can grow.
Anemones wave in a gentle breeze,
While shrimps do backflips with perfect ease.

An octopus hides behind a great rock,
With a wink and a smile, it loves to mock.
The treasures here are not what you think,
It's laughter and fishy pranks with a wink!

A treasure chest full of corny jokes,
And squids that poke with their funny pokes.
In hidden wonders, joy is profound,
With giggles and bubbles all around!

The Great Blue Expanse

In the great blue, a fun game starts,
Where lobsters play darts with their tiny hearts.
A whale serenades with a quirky tune,
While crabs choreograph a dance in the moon.

Fish in tuxedos swim in a race,
Trying to win a trophy made of lace.
The ocean waves bring laughter and cheer,
"Hold on tight!" shouts a fish in a leer.

Starfish count to ten, then they freeze,
As jellyfish float with such graceful ease.
The currents swirl, pulling laughter tight,
As sea turtles giggle in pure delight.

With bubbles that pop and waves that jive,
The great blue expanse keeps dreams alive.
Each splash is a story, each wave has a wish,
Come join the splashes, it's time for a fish!

Lost Treasures of the Tide

Among the shells, the giggles rise,
As sea snails wear their wacky ties.
The tide brings stories of days gone by,
With hidden treasures that make you sigh.

A treasure map, oh what a find!
Only to lead to seaweed and blind.
Mermaids snicker as they gnash their teeth,
While fishy friends trade sweetly wrapped wreaths.

Crabs dig deep looking for gold,
But all they find are stories told.
The tide rolls in with bumps and squeaks,
As laughter echoes for many weeks.

Lost treasures bring more joy than gold,
In the dance of waves, pure laughter unfolds.
With every splash, adventure awaits,
As the ocean hums with funny traits!

Shadows in the Sea

Bubbles float like lunchroom chatter,
Fish play hide and seek, oh what a clatter!
A crab dances with a silly jig,
While a seaweed wig makes the octopus big.

Jellyfish bounce like they own the floor,
While sharks swim by, like they're looking for more.
A clownfish tells jokes that cause quite a stir,
As a sneaky seahorse gives a coy little purr.

A shrimp in a tux, oh what a sight,
Wants to dance but is afraid of the light.
The ocean's a party, oh what a place,
Where laughter and silliness swim with grace.

So come dip your toes in this watery dance,
Where sea creatures twirl in a whimsical trance.
The shadows in the sea shine with delight,
Creating a stage for a watery night.

Tales from the Trench

Deep down where the sunlight's shy,
A fish wears a hat, oh my, oh my!
He tells tall tales of the seaweed's fight,
While sea cucumbers join in, what a sight!

Grouchy crabs grumble, 'It's way too cold!'
As squids spin stories, both funny and bold.
A clam sits quiet, it seems so composed,
But inside, it's laughing—the secret's exposed!

A dolphin named Bob thinks he's quite the star,
Singing off-key about his pet sea guitar.
The anglerfish giggles with light from its bait,
Saying, 'I'm just here to illuminate fate!'

So listen close in the lurking deep,
As the trench keeps secrets that it wants to keep.
With laughter and joy bubbling over the edge,
Each tale from the trench is a funny hedge.

The Heart of the Ocean

In the heart of the ocean where the sea breezes play,
A walrus in glasses reads maps all day.
He thinks he's an explorer, brave and so bold,
But he just found a beach ball—how can he be sold?

Seahorses giggle as they swim round and round,
Dancing to beat of a bubblegum sound.
A sneaky old turtle swims slow with great care,
Stealing everyone's snacks—he just doesn't share!

The heart of the ocean beats soft yet loud,
With fish in a conga line drawing a crowd.
A starfish named Fred thinks he's quite the best,
While sea urchins say, 'Hold on, what a jest!'

So dive into the laughter where the waves splash bright,
With creatures that giggle and jokes that delight.
The heart of the ocean is a whimsical show,
Where friendship and fun make the good times flow.

Voyage of the Unknown

Sailing through waters where fish wear a hat,
A seagull squawks loudly, 'You call that a spat?'
The captain's a turtle, slow but so wise,
Guiding his friends with a gleam in his eyes.

A jellyfish navigator, all floppy and free,
Leads the way through the waves—can't catch him with glee!
The parrotfish sighs, 'I'm just here for the munch,'
While starfish debate who gets the first lunch.

A whale sings loudly, shaking the hull,
Its voice like a foghorn—oh, what a lull!
The ship's made of coral, quite funny to see,
With sea urchins yelling, 'This isn't for me!'

Yet onward they sail into the fun and unknown,
With laughter and mischief, their spirits have grown.
For in the ocean's embrace, joy is the map,
And every wave carries a chuckle or clap.

Messages from the Deep

Bubbles floating up to say,
"Why so blue? It's justP. Play!"
Fish gossip about the current,
"Who's that? An octopus—recurrent!"

Letters written in seaweed script,
Turtles laugh as they take a dip.
Crustaceans in a book club meet,
Sharing tales and salty tweets.

Jellyfish write with flickering gleam,
"Swim this way, it's a great theme!"
All the snails send snail mail too,
Sliding by with a heartfelt "woo!"

Whales on phones make calls in jest,
"Catch you later, I'm off for a quest!"
Underwater texting is the craze,
Sending emojis in fishy ways.

Dance of the Bioluminescent

Glowworms boogie in the deep,
Shaking their tails, bright colors leap.
Dancing with glee in swirling tides,
A rave where every creature hides.

Anglerfish flash their crazy lights,
Inviting pals for late-night bites.
Starfish twirl in their hundred pairs,
Holding hands with curious flares.

The sea cucumber, shy and round,
Takes a chance to join the sound.
"Underwater disco! Join the beat!"
Crabs clap claws in rhythmic heat.

With bubbles popping and laughter free,
It's the party of the deep blue sea!
Every creature shakes with pride,
In the bioluminescent tide.

Tales of the Forgotten Shipwreck

A rusty anchor's tale unfolds,
"Once a pirate, now I'm cold!"
Crabs have claimed the captain's hat,
While rats argue in quiet chat.

Ghostly fish in nets they weave,
"Do we wanna leave or stay?" they grieve.
Treasure chests of glittery shells,
A shop for gossip and fishy spells.

A parrot's squawk from long ago,
"Whichever way the tide will flow!"
Octopus spins a yarn so wild,
About the pirate he once reviled.

With laughter echoing in the blue,
Shipwrecks holding tales anew!
With every tide and wave that crashes,
The ocean keeps our secrets stashed.

Depths of Marine Mystique

Where the clams play hide and seek,
Mysterious waves across the creek.
Anemones giggle, tentacles sway,
Whispers of secrets in the kelp ballet.

The narwhal wears a horn with pride,
"I'm the unicorn! Come, let's glide!"
While dolphins plot their next big prank,
Hiding treasures in the ocean bank.

With each ripple, the secrets grow,
Octopuses spin, putting on a show.
The angelfish winks, a flick of the tail,
In the depths, laughter's always on sale.

So dive on down with a screech and a swim,
The mystique of the sea can make your head swim!
In the blue where giggles collide,
The depths of wonder endlessly abide.

Secrets of the Deep Blue

I met a crab in a fancy hat,
He waved his claws and said, "How about that?"
In the seaweed, a fish danced a jig,
With bubbles trailing, it looked quite big!

A dolphin burst forth, doing a flip,
While a starfish said, "I'll take a dip!"
An octopus offered me a ride,
Then tangled my hair – oh what a ride!

The mermaids laughed, sharing their tales,
Of clumsy sea turtles and oversized snails.
With laughter and splashes, we filled the blue,
Underwater giggles, who knew it was true?

So if you search for a place to play,
Look deep in the ocean, come join the fray!
Laughter and bubbles, what more could you need?
In the secrets of deep blue, let fun be your creed!

Echoes in the Tidal Depths

A fish in a bowtie swam with flair,
Telling tall tales of seasweeps rare.
A jellyfish joined, with a glowing light,
Claiming it glows during a fishy fright!

"Oysters can sing!" sang a clam with glee,
While shrimp played tunes on a seaweed spree.
The whales in the back hummed a merry tune,
Their voices so grand, they scared off the moon!

A seahorse strutted like it was on parade,
Ballet on the sand, oh what a charade!
With every splash, laughter filled the sea,
Echoing stories, floating wild and free.

So dive into chaos, where fun reigns supreme,
In the echoes below, life's just a dream.
Bring your best jokes and your giggly friend,
For in tidal depths, the laughs never end!

Beneath the Surface

Beneath the waves, a party's in place,
With goldfish wearing wigs, what a sight to embrace!
Sea cucumbers dancing, trying to prance,
While crabs tell dad jokes that leave fish in a trance!

A turtle wore shades, looking all cool,
Claiming he's the fastest in this aquatic school.
Clownfish giggled, rolling with glee,
As they tried to squeeze into a plant-shaped marquee!

The anemones waved, feeling quite spry,
While a whale blew bubbles and gave it a try.
With a shimmer of laughter, the ocean swayed,
Beneath the surface, joy was displayed.

So come all ye swimmers with hearts open wide,
In the depths of this ocean, let fun be your guide!
Join in the chaos, where laughter's the key,
Beneath the surface, we're all wild and free!

The Silent Sea Floor

On the silent sea floor, a crab's having tea,
With tales of the currents, his buddies agree.
A sea urchin chimed in with a pointy remark,
While a sleepy old lobster dozed off in the dark!

A fish painted stripes, forgetting the hue,
Surfing on bubbles, oh, what a view!
Clams shared their wisdom, with shells stacked high,
As a sneaky old walrus tried to pass by.

The seafloor was busy with laughter and fuss,
As they flipped and they flopped, creating a fuss!
They turned every stone to uncover the fun,
In a realm where the sun's just a light on the run!

So swing by the depths for a whimsical score,
Where laughter and antics dance evermore!
In the silent sea floor, the fun never fades,
Jump in, make a splash, let silliness cascade!

Whispers Beneath the Waves

Fish in tuxedos, swim by with glee,
Their funky little dances are hard to see.
Jellybeans float and giggle in light,
Making the turtles take off in flight.

Octopus plays cards, no bluff in his game,
He always wins, but who's really to blame?
Clownfish chuckle at bubbles that burst,
While seaweed sways to a tune that's rehearsed.

Crabs wear top hats, parade in a line,
Declaring that seaweed is totally fine.
Starfish gossip about sunken ships,
As dolphins laugh, doing silly flips.

Underwater parties, they never complain,
With sea cucumbers dancing in the rain.
So dive down deep, where the fun never ends,
In this wacky world where the ocean pretends.

Echoes of the Abyss

In the dark deep, where shadows roam free,
A whale serenades, as loud as can be.
Barnacles gossip on rocks made of pearl,
While sea horses strut in a merry whirl.

One fish declares he's discovered a sun,
While others just giggle, "That's simply not fun!"
A ghost crab with shades, strutting with flair,
Says, "Underwater, it's all about the hair!"

The inkfish paints murals upon ocean walls,
Each stroke, a laugh, as the water enthralls.
A deep-sea diva sways with such pride,
Saying, "Oh darling, watch this tide!"

Echoes of laughter through currents so fast,
Make each moment a treasure that's meant to last.
So swim down and twirl, let your worries erase,
In the depths full of jokes, find your happy place.

The Siren's Call

A siren's voice, a cheeky surprise,
With fishy puns and wink-filled eyes.
She beckons the sailors to dive right in,
But beware her laughter, it's quite a din!

Mermaids juggling pearls, such a fine show,
While seahorses sip on their fancy sea flow.
"Stop right there!" shouts a clam with a grin,
"Those jokes are a riot, can I join in?"

Her fellow sea creatures break into a cheer,
With a bubble machine that spreads so much cheer.
Even the sea urchins can't help but grin,
As they bounce along, ready to join in.

So heed the siren, but don't take a fall,
In this funny tale of the ocean's great hall.
For in every giggle that bubbles and sways,
Is a whimsical world that forever stays.

Luminous Below

In waters aglow with a neon-lit show,
Fishes wear shades, always ready to go.
Glowing algae dance, twinkling like stars,
While clams play the drums in their oceanic bars.

Anemones giggle, tickling passing fish,
While sea turtles argue, "What's for our dish?"
Sardines in formations are quite the proud crew,
As they spin and twirl, creating a view.

Deep in the blue, where the quirky reside,
A narwhal dons glasses, takes all in stride.
"Who needs the sun?" laughs a bright anglerfish,
"Down here we have fun, that's our only wish!"

With laughter and light, the ocean ignites,
Where fun-loving critters have marvelous nights.
So down in the depths, let your heart feel the glow,
In this lively kingdom, where joy steals the show.

Encounters with Ocean Giants

Down in the deep where the big fish roam,
I met a whale who claimed to be home.
With a wink of his eye and a flip of his tail,
He said, "Watch for sharks, they love to snail!"

A turtle named Shelly wore a bright hat,
She thought she was clever, but oh, imagine that!
With a wink and a nudge, she tripped on some sand,
"Next time I swim, I'll plan my land!"

A dolphin danced by, with acrobatic flair,
Said, "Come learn my moves, they're beyond compare!"
But as I tried jumping, I flipped on my face,
Now I'm the clown in this watery space!

Among the sea cucumbers, bright and aloof,
There's gossip of mermaids and their hidden roof.
But when I asked for a ticket to see,
They laughed and said, "You just can't be free!"

Ocean's Veil of Mystery

Bubbles I chased with a giggle and whirl,
In the depths of the sea, where the seaweed would swirl.
A fish in a bowtie said, "You're quite a sight!"
"Join our disco, we dance every night!"

Seaweed got tangled in my hair like a mess,
I looked like a lady in a green, tedious dress.
The crab gave a chuckle and said, "What's the style?"
"Came for the ocean, but stayed for the guile!"

An octopus winked with his eight funny arms,
Stretched out to toast with humorous charms.
"We raise a glass to this curious fate,
Life's much funnier when you just levitate!"

A jellyfish floated, glowing so bright,
Declared, "I'm the glowstick of every sea night!"
But when he tripped over coral too slick,
We laughed so hard, it was truly a kick!

Below the Surface: A Realm Apart

In a realm where the gloomy meets the bright,
I found a clam with a pearl of pure light.
He said, "Keep it secret, it's for good luck,
But don't try to eat, or you'll end up stuck!"

The starfish had style, wearing shades from the store,
"I'm the trendsetter, who could ask for more?"
But slipping on kelp in a move so slick,
He fell like a star, it was quite the trick!

Beneath colorful corals, the sea was a chat,
A pufferfish puffed and burst like a brat.
"It's just my defense; I'm not trying to scare!"
But the laughter erupted, filling the air!

A lionfish strutted, all spines and all pride,
"Come follow me, let's take a fun ride!"
But he led us in circles, and we got so dizzy,
"Let's call it a day, I'm feeling quite fizzy!"

Sunken Dreams of the Horizon

Amidst the wrecks where the stories unfold,
I found a goldfish, with treasures retold.
"I guard all the secrets from sailors long lost,
But by all means, I'm not a fan of frost!"

Diving through ruins, a treasure I sought,
But found only bubbles, not gold that I thought.
A seagull swooped down with a caw so absurd,
"This isn't the place for a dream of a bird!"

Coral castles stood tall with a whimsical flair,
While sea urchins giggled from their prickly lair.
"If you're looking for dreams, you might just find none,
But we serve great laughs; come on, let's have fun!"

A narwhal took charge, with his horn held up high,
"Let's set sail for laughter under the sky!"
But when he dived down, we all lost our seats;
We surfaced in chaos—what a trip to the beats!

www.ingramcontent.com/pod-product-compliance
Lightning Source LLC
Chambersburg PA
CBHW060146230426
43661CB00003B/591